RHYTHM PART 8

BY: P.LANE

Abortion

By: P.Lane

The phrase "A woman's right to choose…"

Has been all over the news

"My body, my choice!"

On this topic, women have had a loud voice

"The male politicians telling us what to do!" They scream

Republicans like Bush or Democrats like Howard Dean

All points need to be seen

Then, we need to make an agreement and be clean

But, where do I stand?

What side does P.Lane command

I lean Pro-choice, but I'm damned if I do or if I don't

But, I'm not all " You baby killer!" Or religious like the Pope

I'm also Pro-Choice under another condition

That a required paternity test be made so the wrong man ain't paying child support or going to Prison

Women's Rights, OK

Men's Rights, same say

True Equality today

For that, I pray

I'm not either politically left or right

But, this will be an ongoing fight

Both sides will use might

No end in sight

I could be wrong, I don't know

I'm not always thinking I'm right for show

It's not all glamorous to give birth like they show in pop-culture

When a mom, you have to do your job like a circling vulture

Watch your kids like a hawk

While in Washington, they argue and talk

About abortion

Is it a crime of great proportions?

Does it anger a higher power

Should you cancel that baby shower?

Should you give it up for adoption straight away?

Would you regret terminating the life for many more days?

Or months…years? Whatever…

We're really gonna debate this forever…

Just do what you feel is right

Roe vs. Wade won't be overturned tonight

Maybe your Pro-choice or Pro-life

Whatever just smile and be bright!

Censorship

By: P.Lane

It is what it is

What's that fizz?

It is what it is

What's that fizz?

His language had a bad leap

Let's do a bleep

He talks like a freak

Let's do a bleep

Is it to protect the kids?

Or attacking free speech and trying to control show biz?

Censorship is what people hate

No matter polite, or angry and irate

Protect the kids, what they see or hear

If my son swears, I won't get honored mom of the year

It's for their safety and protection

There are bad influences in every direction

Rate the games, movies

Hide the truth of the violence and nudities

Oh and lets all have stupid, politically correct terms

That we all gotta learn

Say it or burn racist burn!

Oh, for the pure days we yearn

But, I doubt we can go back

And we can't just go to rehab for this habit like you can for crack

These are the times

When censors are fine

Mature video games?   Not on my dime!

Remember, protecting you is at the front of the line!

You've got no say on what can and can't be said

I don't want you to think or use your head

Connor at 17

By: P.Lane

Brother is 17 today

I don't know what he's thinking or has to say

But he went out, had some fun bowling with friends

Went out to a pizza place, had a good time til the end

Then, he played video games

Good times, good days

February 5, 1993

Was when he came through mom's tummy

February 5, 2010

Was when he conquered life over and over again

He just kept being Connor and can now beat me up

When the World made him, they had good luck

He's got more hair on his body than anyone at his school

But, he still rules

Happy birthday bro

Sports Poem #4

By: P.Lane

The Saints just won the Game

They beat the Colts it was insane

Whether shine or rain

They lit up Miami and the World all the same

There was Magic Johnson of the Lakers in the 1980s

He and Larry Bird dueled like women over their babies

Then there's the guys that hit the golf ball

Will Tiger Woods come out tall?

Small?

Or will his adultery be his downfall?

There's the sportscasters

They report the best plays and biggest disasters

Charles Barkley is the master

Baseball season 2010

Watch with reason, yet again

The Winter Olympics are soon

They don't have that in June

Vancouver, Canada is the host

What Sports moment do you like most?

What Sports, what kind or athlete do you like3?

Would you see Wayne Gretzky on ice?

Or Lance Armstrong on a bike?

What would be more nice?

Would you see Usain Bolt on the Track?

Venus Williams' tennis ball take a whack?

Michael Phelps swim there and back?

Or is Basketball your knack?

Want Michael, Lebron or Kobe with that?

How bout a Shaq Attack?

Or are you amazed

By Football Plays

Could be American or World

David Beckham likes the Spice girls

There's good games

Everywhere these days

Follow who wins, who loses, who's benched and who plays

Who knows what the Coach at halftime says

Bad Teacher

By: P.Lane

A bad teacher can't do or teach

A bad teacher's students can't reach

A bad teacher is a leach

For all a bad teacher will preach

A bad teacher is biased

A bad teacher yells and tells their kids to be quiet

A bad teacher snaps

A bad teacher abuses Kindergartners while they take a nap

A bad teacher goes to jail for abuse

A bad teacher lies

A bad teacher intrudes

In your space and life like flies

13

A bad teacher gives you an F

A bad teacher gives you impossible tests

A bad teacher is usually sneaky

A bad teacher is rarely punished which is freaky

A bad teacher plays favorites then denies it later

A bad teacher is an individuality hater

A bad teacher punishes you for late Homework

A bad teacher always tells you you're the jerk

But it was the bad teacher the entire time

I hate bad teachers they are swine

Good Teacher

By: P.Lane

A good teacher is patient

A good teacher is a truth and learning agent

A good teacher has knowledge and power

A good teacher is one you want to shower with love and flowers

A good teacher works with you and won't let you fail

A good teacher sends out emails

A good teacher isn't slow like a snail

A good teacher has wit that will make you turn red from pale

A good teacher is funny

A good teacher is sunny

A good teacher is still learning

A good teacher is fire burning

15

a good teacher isn't shy

A good teacher asks "why?"

A good teacher isn't a jerk

A good teacher never overloads you with work

A good teacher is smart

A good teacher has a heart

A good teacher wishes his students the best

A good teacher is one who students still talk to when they're in grade next

A good teacher is relaxed

A good teacher can normally add and subtract

A good teacher cares

A good teacher is there

A good teacher stands out from the rest

A good teacher is among the best

A good teachers' spirit is never mean

A good teacher lets' his students dream

Those Girls

By: P.Lane

Those girls whispering in each other's ears

Those College Girls and their beer

Those girls stealing boyfriends

Those girls speaking ill of best friends

Those girls in a Sorority House

Those girls sneaky as a mouse

Those girls that talk when you aren't around

Those girls who pack on the pounds

Those girls who make their rounds

Those Softball girls on the mound

Those Cheerleaders make peppy sounds

Those girls who criticize and nag

Those girls who show off and brag

Those girls who are rich

The girls who are a bitch

Those girls you want to take home to mama

Those girls that like too much drama

Those girls that are shallow like Hal

Those girls who are your pals

Those girls who mostly hang with guys

Those girls at McDonalds serving fries

Those girls who know martial arts

Those girls who kick guys in the parts

Those girls who are single moms

Those girls who are snobs

Those girls who model

Those girls who run cross country with water bottles

Those girls at the gym

Those catty girls who have to win

Those girls with the good grades

Those girls that don't behave

Those girls kissing at the club

Those girls you love

Those girls you carry to the sea

Those girls you ask "will you marry me?"

Those Guys

By: P.Lane

Those guys that roughhouse

Those guys that kill that mouse

Those guys that like Sports

Those guys that are dorks

Those guys in jail

Those guys at Yale

Those guys that drink

Those guys that stink

Those guys that are corny

Those guys that are horny

Those guys with cheesy pick up lines

Those guys who save lives

Those guys who lie

Those guys are shy

Those guys that get those girls pregnant

Those guys gawking at the girls in the beauty pageant

Those guys have big muscles

Those guys get into tussles

Those guys playing basketball at the park

Those guys partying at dark

Those guys in a Fraternity bid

Those guys that should shut their lid

Those guys that are nice

With girls those guys will pay the price

Those guys that cheat

Those guys that you always meet

Those guys that are manly

Those guys that love their family

Those guys that like other men

Those guys at 30, still living in their parents den

Those guys that play video games

Those guys that get called names

Those guys that have the power

Those guys that need to shower

Those guys…those guys..those guys…

Vampire Life

By: P.Lane

I live a Vampire Life

I am asleep in the day, awake at night

Love the dark, hate the bright

And the sunlight

If that says anything about me…

I wish people would just let P.Lane be

No social interactions

No drama, no infractions

Just me, my dog, my caffeine and internet

Dracula's fang's are wet

Nah…blood is gross

So, I can't be a Vampire but in all seriousness I like being a night owl the most

Big Baby

By: P.Lane

I am basically a big baby

But, I've grown up a lot lately

To my credit

All you are jealous

Of this big baby

I am irresponsible, immature

I laugh like a lunatic for sure

I cry and I'm a grown man

I live day by day, reading tabloids from lalaland

I get yelled at much

I'm like a kid whose parents' didn't bring him lunch

I live at my dad's house eating chicken nuggets

I've worn my mom's blouse in public

I call my brother names

I wonder if I use enough brains

At least I'm self aware

Wrote this poem, I dared

I'm too immature for a girlfriend

I'm too immature for the World times 10

OK I exaggerated just then

But still is it if I grow up or when

That's how society sees it

But, I do what I want so be it

You know it

I'm P.Lane, the poet

I burp, I fart

I ask my dad too much if I'm smart

I sound annoying don't I

C'mon ladies, I'm the perfect boyfriend don't be shy

They say men are irresponsible these days

Well maybe, maybe not but I'm the king in every way

I just sit at home, play online

For most only me, do I have time

Could you live with P.Lane

Or would he make you insane

Like a train

Hitting your membrane

It lowers me in society's eyes

But, in my mind, I'm a prize

As long as I've got self esteem

As long as I'm allowed to daydream

As long as I'm King and Big Gulps are my Queen

As long as you don't nag me to go to the shallow bar scene

Basically, As long as you let me be immature

I will love you for sure

Just Married!

By: P.Lane

Glorious day this is

I'm going to marry Big Gulps gee whiz

Have a cake

And celebrate

The wedding of P.Lane

I know he's crazy in the brain!

He drinks Big Gulps shine or rain!

Makes the soda fountains drain

I married Big Gulps bitch!

I just got hitched!

This is my drink, my bride!

This is my wife, my pride!

I'm alive

Cause I don't drink and drive

Big Gulps are my spouse

I wear the pants in this house

No one challenges P.Lane's authority not even Eric Cartman

Cause P.Lane's just to smart of a man!

His dad, his brother

His family, his dead mother

Who he looked up to in Heaven on this glorious day

To say

Haha! You ain't invited babay!

Now get out of my way!

She already was, she was up in the sky

P.Lane and his Big Gulp went swimming at the Y

He kissed her and wasn't ever shy

They would be together until one would die

30

The End

93%

By: P.Lane

93% of communication is non-verbal, reading body language has its perks

Is it really? Or are reading more dribble from "experts"

If it's true

Why are we that judgmental, me and you?

It's good to be wary

But, we don't trust each other, that's scary

Reading body language, It's something I can hardly do

Probably because of Autism features, yes it's true

I don't judge you most of the time

I don't now, or when I was 9

"Body Language" to me is nonsense

How do they know what I think? Some people are a mental mess

How is a man supposed to "pass a woman's tests"

If he's not a non-verbal communication excess

So, I can't read body cues

Oh, the blues

This was made news

So, those non-verbal people like me can "give up and lose"

When I found this "fact" out

It was so dumb, I wanted to shout

Golly, it's too dumb to be true

All these unimportant "facts" from "studies" just shoo!

All the people who can't read minds

Just sit back, and laugh hard at this lie

If people don't listen and expect you to "read" them

Then, you don't need them

Also, if people are that judgmental

Then, I love the curly hair on Shirley Temple

Oh, wait I'll never love that

But, just know that figure is quite likely too high and crap

Burgers

By: P.Lane

I just at burgers and cheese

It tastes way better than vegetables and peas

I'm a meat-eater at heart

Was now, and from the start

The meat you taste after it's been grilled

Makes your taste buds no less than thrilled

It's like Homer Simpson would say

"MMM BURGERS!" Ok?

It's good for lunch, breakfast and dinner

If you it in you're a winner

If you don't, that's fine too

I'll disagree with you

Vegans I'm sure knew

That burgers would bring you happy from the blues

Don't choke on it

Keep on eating, don't quit

It's got buns

It's got yums

It's got meat

A treat

It's got cheese

More please

Then other toppings

What's stopping

You from throwing on the sauce

You the boss

Pickles or tomatoes

More for extra topping, you'll pay more though

Mayo, ketchup

Your blesses with a burger, don't mess-up

Go to McDonalds, the store

Be rich or poor

If you've got a pulse you should want more

Burgers

"It's a nice gig"

By: P.Lane

It's a nice gig if you can get it

If you have a job and can quit it

Ride the gravy train

Shine or rain

Try to stay sane

Study Philosophy, use your brain

Don't live to please others, just you

As long as your respectful do what you wanna do

I don't wanna go to work all the time

My World ain't a companies' it's mine!

Please, I'll be fine

I'll just chill and have soda instead of wine

I don't drink

I face it all and think

If I wanna hit the store, I can

Thank God I had a helping hand

I don't take orders from a superior

But, I'm far from inferior

Society may see me as a bum

They may think I'm dumb

I'm not either of those and I think I'll go far

That'll make some skeptics scar

It's a nice gig, if you can get it

Most people can't thought, they hate their jobs, the Americans, Canada, China and the British

Why work my ass off all day?

I'll do what I may!

I've read the Hunters-Gatherers worked 8 hours a week

It was slow-paced back then and didn't reek

Of stress

But, sometimes there was a mess

A Saber-toothed tiger they had to kill

A mudslide spill

But life was very simple back in that day

They weren't trying to get money in every way

It's a good gig if you have fun

And aren't trying to be the best and having everyone outrun

Lay in the sun

Drop the competition hun

Life's good to me

Just let me be

It's a good gig

Problem is…can you get it?

Withholding sex

By: P.Lane

Honey, what about my needs?

I'm tired, go away please!

But, you said when you'd be home, I'd get some action!

Well, take that promise and do subtraction!

Honey, do you have a headache too?

No, I'm just tired of sex addicts like you.

Why, am I a bad lover in bed?

No, you just think with the wrong head

Baby, little or big one?

You know, and with that attitude, it'll be awhile before we have fun

C'mon baby, don't deny me!

I know your horny, but let me be

Lets make a sex time some time!

No thanks, I'm fine

C'mon, my little head wants some!

Shut-up, or your sleeping on the couch, god you're dumb!

Maybe with your attitude, it would be good if I did!

Stop bugging me! Shut your lid!

C'mon, doggy style!

Trust me, It's gonna be awhile

Missionary!

Your scaring me!

C'mon, lets do the dirty

Shut-up! Tomorrow I gotta go to work early!

Are you having an affair?

Alright, I'm sitting over there

I'll follow you and keep pestering

Shut-up, stop lecturing!

I just wanna get in your pants

Well, then do a dance

What! No, I'm not gay baby it's time for romance!

Boy, you're in a sexual trance

I'm gonna kiss you

Then you'll be on the couch and I won't miss you

I forgot! It's that time of the month!

Boy, you are really a dunce

What can I say, I'm in love

Aw, gimme a hug

Yeah, I like a little cuddlin' that's right!

Well, good night!

Sleep tight!

Stop staring at me, I'm gonna turn off the lights!

There. Let's make love, not fight

Art

By: P.Lane

Da Vinci, Michelangelo

Raphael, Donatello

The Super-Turtles and Renaissance Artists, here we go!

Michelangelo worked for the Medici's

The Mona Lisa would make good graffiti

Art means something different to everyone

Water color that, son!

There's Picasso

Andy Warhol

There's drawings, painings

Art is in stadiums and in churches where they do Saintings

Hold still, here's your portrait

Art is beautiful, unlike horse shit

I love sculptures too

What do Art museums do for you

Sketches to create

Much Art to appreciate

Art is beautiful

Art is cool

Art is not for fools

Art makes rules

I used to think Art is feminine, boy I was wrong

I love Art like the sight of a good thong

Art makes comic books

Art is good to collect, has good looks

Art's makers sadly starve

Trying to sell a painting or sculpture they carved

Ipod

By: P.Lane

I got my ipod with me

I'll get the device in a jiffy

I'll play the songs loudly

I will listen proudly

To the certain bands, instruments, sounds

It's exciting and good to have found

This gadget. It makes me "cooler" to be around

Pound for pound

The ipod is cooler

Then the computer

Just kidding, but it is cuter

Plus, you have music sooner

Just watch it so it can't be stolen

48

Don't drop it so it can't be broken

When I see a guy with an Ipod, I say what's up

He says's not much

Then we go about our business

But, I bore witness

To that device

Called "Ipod" They are very nice

I got in at an Apple Store

Back then, it wasn't for the poor

Hundreds of dollars was the price

But, it was nice

To have an Ipod

Author Bio

Patrick Lane is a newly Published Author out of Arizona. Throughout life, he has lived With Tourettes and Aspergers Syndrome but hasn't let it hold him back. He travels with His family several times annually, plays sports, runs in races from 4 miles to a marathon And is training gradually for an Ultramarathon sometime in 2010. Patrick, 22, can also Be seen constantly walking, running and biking around Tempe, Arizona. He is a 2006 Graduate of Corona Del Sol High School and attended Mesa Community College. His Passion is writing and wishes to do that for a living.

www.ingramcontent.com/pod-product-compliance
Lightning Source LLC
Chambersburg PA
CBHW081241090426
42738CB00016B/3374